WHAT IS A FISH?

Robert Snedden

Photographs by Oxford Scientific Films

Illustrated by Adrian Lascom

Sierra Club Books for Children
San Francisco

For Christopher

The Sierra Club, founded in 1892 by John Muir, has devoted itself to the study and protection of the earth's scenic and ecological resources — mountains, wetlands, woodlands, wild shores and rivers, deserts and plains. The publishing program of the Sierra Club offers books to the public as a nonprofit educational service in the hope that they may enlarge the public's understanding of the Club's basic concerns. The Sierra Club has some sixty chapters in the United States and in Canada. For information about how you may participate in its programs to preserve wilderness and the quality of life, please address inquiries to Sierra Club, 85 Second Street, San Francisco, CA 94105.

First Paperback Edition 1997

First published in Great Britain in 1993 by Belitha Press Limited, London House, Great Eastern Wharf, Parkgate Road, London SW11 4NQ

Library of Congress Cataloging-in-Publication Data

Snedden, Robert.
      What is a fish?/Robert Snedden;
photographs by Oxford Scientific Films; illustrated by Adrian Lascom.
      p.   cm.
      Includes index.
      Summary: Describes different types of fish, their breathing, movement, senses, food, defenses, and birth.
      ISBN 0-87156-545-5 (hc)
      ISBN 0-87156-924-8 (pb)
      1. Fishes—Juvenile literature. [1. Fishes.]
I. Lascom, Adrian, ill. II. Oxford Scientific Films. III. Title.
QL617.2.S64
597—dc20   93-6495

Printed in Portugal
10 9 8 7 6 5 4 3 2 1

Editor: Rachel Cooke
Designer: Frances McKay
Consultant: Dr. Jim Flegg
Educational consultant: Brenda Hart

The publisher wishes to thank the following for permission to reproduce copyrighted material:

Oxford Scientific Films and individual copyright holders on the following pages: Fred Bavendam, 6; Fredrik Ehrenstrom, 24 top; Max Gibbs, cover, title page, contents page, 4, 5 bottom, 12 bottom, 17; Laurence Gould, 16; Howard Hall, 8 bottom; Pam and Willy Kemp, 18/19; Breck P. Kent/Animals Animals, 10/11, 27 top; Rudie Kuiter, 5 top, 13 bottom, 20 inset, 26; Zig Leszczynski/Animals Animals, 7 center and bottom, 14, 24 center and bottom; Colin Milkins, 9 bottom; Tsuneo Nakamura, 25 top; J. E. Paling, 7 top; Peter Parks, 13 center, 27 bottom; Robert Redden/Animals Animals, 8 top right; Kathy Tyrrell, 20/21; P. and W. Ward, 25 bottom; W. Wisniewski/Okapia, 11 top; Norbert Wu, 15.

Front cover:
A coral trout.

Title page: Clown loaches, such as this one, are found in the rivers of Indonesia.

Contents page: The purple surgeonfish lives in the Red Sea.

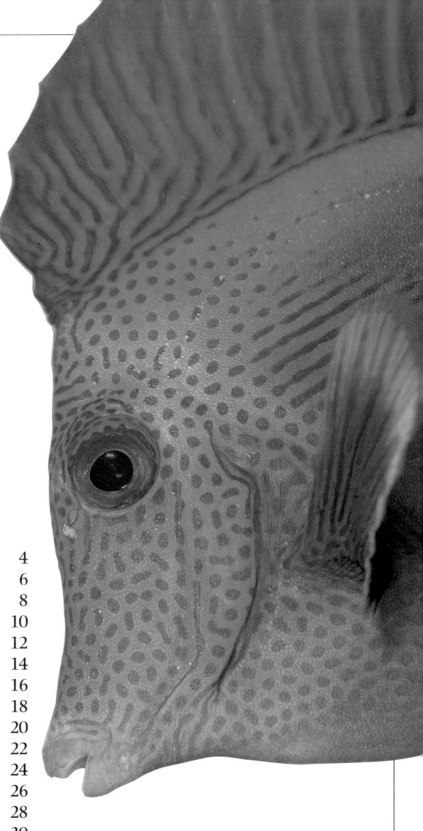

CONTENTS

WHAT IS A FISH?

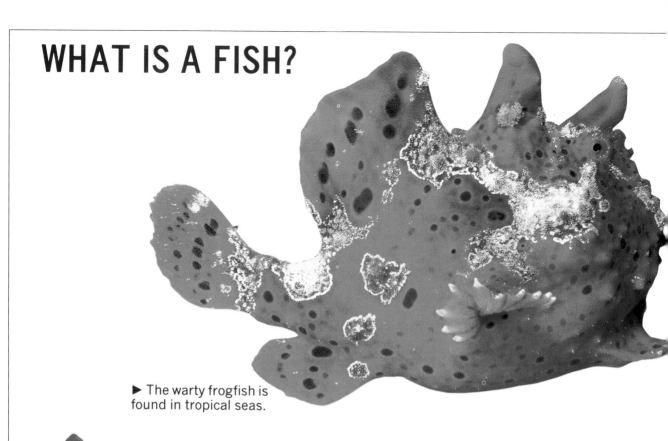

▶ The warty frogfish is found in tropical seas.

What do you think of when you think of a fish? You probably think of a brightly colored animal flashing quickly through the water. You might even think of something to eat!

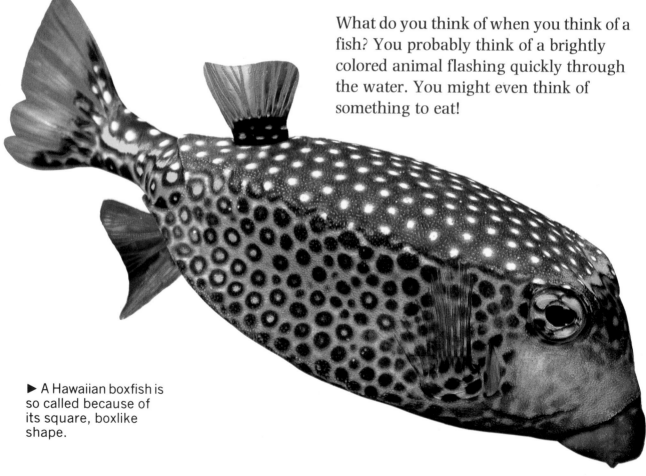

▶ A Hawaiian boxfish is so called because of its square, boxlike shape.

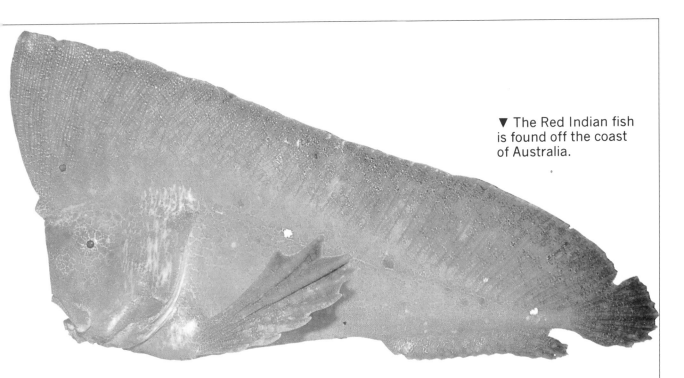

▼ The Red Indian fish is found off the coast of Australia.

Fish come in a huge variety of shapes, sizes and colors. They range from the extraordinary Red Indian fish to the jigsaw triggerfish; from the Hawaiian boxfish darting through the coral to the bright red warty frogfish gliding through the ocean.

Yet all fish have certain things in common. These things make them different from the other animals that live in the oceans, lakes and rivers of the world. We shall be looking at some of them in this book.

▼ The jigsaw triggerfish lives on the Great Barrier Reef off the Australian coast.

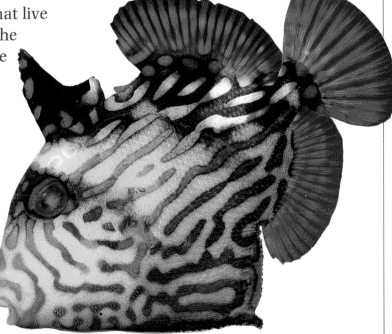

TYPES OF FISH

There are three main types of fish. First there are the **jawless fish**. These include lampreys and hagfish. They have smooth, slimy skin. They can't swim very well and move by thrashing around. Their mouths tend to be like suckers with lots of small teeth. They feed by attaching themselves to other fish and rasping away their flesh with their teeth.

The second main group of fish are the sharks and rays. Their skin is covered with rough scales. If you stroked a shark it would feel like sandpaper. Most sharks and rays are excellent swimmers that live by catching and eating other animals. They do not have **skeletons** made of bone inside their bodies. Instead, their skeletons are made of a gristle-like tissue called **cartilage**, as are the skeletons of the jawless fish. Cartilage is tough and flexible.

▼ The spotted wobbegong shark is part of the group of fish whose skeletons are made of cartilage rather than bone.

◄ A river lamprey, a type of jawless fish, feeding on a trout, which is a bony fish.

▼ A sea lamprey, showing its sucker mouth.

The biggest group of fish are the **bony fish**. As you would guess from the name, their skeletons are made of bone like those of reptiles, birds and mammals. Their skin is covered by smooth scales. There are four times as many different types of bony fish as there are other types of fish. We will look at some other differences between bony fish and other fish later.

Whichever group of fish they belong to, all fish have certain things in common. They all have **gills** to allow them to breathe in water, and they all have **fins** that help them to swim in the water.

A Moorish idol, a colorful bony fish. ►

BREATHING UNDERWATER

In order to live, all animals must have a gas called **oxygen**. Animals that live on land can breathe in oxygen from the air around them. How do fish, which live underwater, manage to get oxygen?

Fish use the oxygen that is dissolved in the water. To get this oxygen fish have to move the water over their gills. Every fish has gills on both sides of its head. Gills do the same job as your **lungs**.

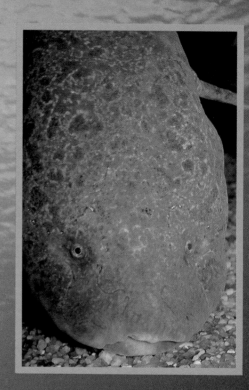

▶ An African lungfish gets most of the oxygen it needs by breathing air rather than water.

▼ This reef shark's gill slits can be seen just behind its head.

The fish takes in water through its mouth in the same way as you breathe in air. This water then passes over its gills. The oxygen in the water moves into the blood in the fish's gills. The oxygen you breathe into your lungs moves into your blood in the same way. The water is then pumped back out from the gills. Bony fish have flaps to protect their gills, and these open to let the water out. Sharks and rays don't have gill flaps. They have gill slits that open as the water flows through.

There are actually fish that can breathe in oxygen from the air. These are called lungfish. They have gills, just like any other fish, but they also have lungs, just like land-living animals. They live in lakes and marshes in Africa, Australia and South America. Sometimes their homes dry up in summer, but the lungfish can survive by burying themselves in the mud and breathing air. When the rain comes again, the lakes fill up and the lungfish can use their gills in the water once more.

Whales and dolphins are not fish, even though they live in the sea all the time. They don't have gills but lungs. They can stay underwater for a very long time but must come to the surface eventually to breathe air. Whales and dolphins are, in fact, mammals, as are humans.

▼ The cutaway diagram shows the structure of a bony fish's gills. The gills extract oxygen from the water passing over them, moving it into the fish's blood.

▼ ▼ The photograph (bottom) shows how a bony fish's gills are protected by gill flaps.

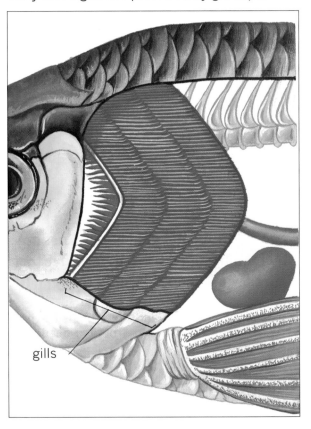

gills

Did you know?

Most fish breathe by opening and shutting their mouths gently to get water flowing over their gills. Some sharks, however, just swim along with their mouths open all the time.

HEARING UNDERWATER

At first glance, fish don't appear to have any ears. In fact, for a long time people thought that fish couldn't hear at all. But fish do have ears, and most can hear very well. It's because fish don't have outer ears like you do that they look as if they don't have ears. The flaps on the sides of your head that you call ears are really just the outside parts that help pick up sounds.

Humans have an **eardrum** inside each ear. The sound enters the ear and makes the eardrum vibrate. This vibration is passed on to the part of the ear where the sound is heard.

Fish don't have eardrums. In fact, the ears of most fish don't have openings to the outside at all. A fish's ears are protected inside **capsules** on both sides of its head, just behind its eyes. Sound travels very well through water, better than it does through air. A fish's body, like that of all animals, contains a great deal of water. Sound can travel straight through the fish's body to its ears, where it is heard.

Many types of fish can pick up sounds in another way. Their ears are joined to their swim bladders. The walls of the swim bladder are made to vibrate by the sound traveling through the water, just like an eardrum is vibrated by sound traveling through the air. This vibration is then passed to the fish's ears, usually along a chain of small bones that join them to the swim bladder. Some kinds of fish have tubes (rather than bones) that extend from the swim bladder forward to the ear capsules.

► Fish's ears are covered, but they can still hear very well. They also make many different noises. This trunkfish can growl like a dog!

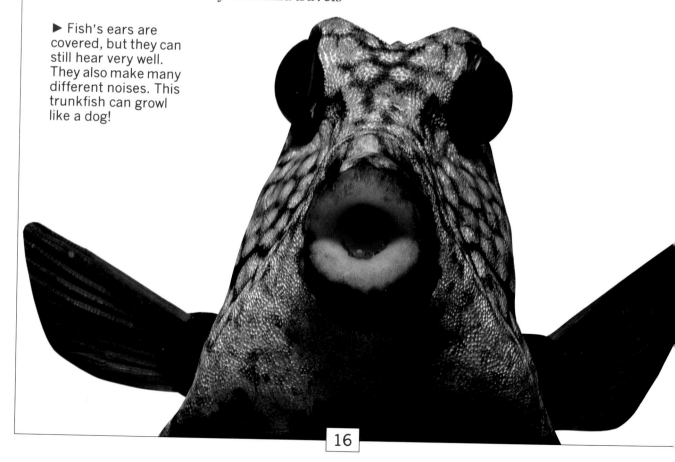

▲ Catfish can make noises by using special drumming muscles that vibrate their swim bladders.

► Loaches can make squeaking noises like mice by blowing air from their swim bladders.

Fish often communicate by making noises. Many fish can make powerful calls to one another that can be heard many miles away. Some types of fish make noise by grinding their teeth together, others by rubbing their fins against their bodies. Many fish can use their swim bladders to make sounds as well as to detect them. Special drumming muscles vibrate the swim bladder to make the sounds.

Did you know?

Many fish are very noisy eaters. This means that if one fish finds something to eat, very soon lots of other fish will hear it and come to join in.

A toadfish can be almost as loud as an underground train! It makes a noise to attract female toadfish and to warn off any rival males.

TASTING AND SMELLING

Mammals and birds taste mainly with their tongues, but some kinds of fish can taste with their whole bodies! The parts of you that do the tasting are called **taste buds**, and these are found mostly on your tongue. A fish's taste buds are not only in its mouth but also around its head and pectoral fins and even on its body.

Some fish, such as cod and catfish, have long feelers around their mouths. These are called **barbels**, and they have taste buds, too. The fish uses them to find food hidden in muddy river or lake bottoms.

Fish have nostrils on their heads that they use for smelling just like other large animals. They never use their nostrils to breathe through. Sharks have an incredibly good sense of smell. They can detect the blood of a wounded fish or other animal in the water from a great distance.

Salmon spend the first part of their lives in rivers but as adults live in the ocean. They always return to the river where they were born to lay and **fertilize** their eggs. They find the right river by remembering how it smelled and tasted.

When injured, some fish make a smell to warn other fish. If the skin of a minnow is broken—perhaps when it is bitten by another fish—it produces an alarm substance. Other minnows smell this and swim away from the danger.

◄ The smell of blood often attracts large numbers of sharks. Their excellent sense of smell leads sharks quickly to food.

FISH SENSES

As well as being able to see, smell, taste and hear, fish have special senses of their own. Along each side of their bodies, just under the skin, most fish have a line of sensitive detectors that can pick up the slightest movement of the water around them. These are called **lateral lines**.

Tiny pores or pits in the skin along the lateral lines are open to the water. These let the fish feel any slight difference in **pressure** along its body. It can use this information to tell from which direction a disturbance is coming.

Lateral line detectors on a fish's head can tell the fish if it is about to swim into something by enabling the fish to feel the water pushing against the object. This is why you almost never see a fish swim into the glass wall of a fish tank.

Fish that live in large groups, called **schools** or **shoals**, may use their lateral line sense as well as their sight to avoid

If you look carefully at this perch you can see its lateral line running along the middle of its body. ▶

colliding with one another. Sometimes when a shoal is attacked, the fish flash off in all directions. Each fish could be traveling twenty times its own length in a second. But they never collide!

Some fish can detect tiny **electric currents** in the water. Dogfish can find the fish they eat even when they are buried in the sand at the bottom of the sea. The muscles of all animals produce tiny amounts of electricity when they work.

The dogfish can detect this electricity coming from other fish.

Electric eels and some other fish have special muscles that can produce large amounts of electricity. This electricity is powerful enough to stun other animals. Electric eels can also use their electricity to find their way about in the murky water where they live. They do this by sensing the way the electric current spreads through the water.

Fish such as this school of sardines can swim together in large groups without colliding with one another. ▼

FISH FOOD

If there is something in the water that can be eaten, then it is almost certain that somewhere there is a fish that can eat it!

There are fish that eat plants and fish that eat other fish; just as on land there are animals that eat plants and animals that eat other animals. Many river fish will eat the plants that grow along the river's edge. There are fish that will eat the simple plants called **algae** that often grow on rocks.

In the ocean many fish live by mainly eating **plankton**. Plankton are tiny plants and animals that float in the water. The biggest fish of all, whale sharks and basking sharks, live on plankton. They have special mouth parts called **gill-rakers**. These strain the tiny plankton out of the water before it passes through their gills. Other fish that feed on plankton also have gill-rakers.

Most fish are **carnivores**. This means that they eat other animals – including other fish! The teeth of some kinds of fish are joined together into sharp-edged

▲ The great white shark's teeth are a special kind of scale. They are excellent tools for this active hunter.

▲ Angelfish have strong jaws and teeth to cut through the coral that they eat.

gill-rakers

plates. These are fish that
feed on hard coral or hard-shelled
shellfish, such as oysters and mussels.

Others, such as many sharks and tuna,
are fast, active hunters. Sharks' teeth are
unlike those of other fish. They are, in fact,
a special kind of scale. A shark has several
rows of teeth in its jaw, lying one behind
the other. Usually only the row of teeth at
the front is actually in use. As these teeth
are worn or damaged they are replaced by
the teeth behind them. They provide a
powerful cutting edge.

Sharks have teeth only in their jaws,
but bony fish can have teeth on their
tongues and in their throats, as well as
along their jaws. Many fish have strong,
sharply pointed teeth that they use to
catch their prey.

Some types of fish have jaws that can
open up enormously. In the deepest parts
of the ocean there may not be very much
to eat. This means that it is important to be
able to eat anything that is found. Some
deep-sea fish have jaws and bellies that
can stretch so much they can actually
swallow fish that are bigger than they are!

▲ A basking shark's
gill-rakers strain the
plankton that they eat
from the water.

▶ River fish such as
these goldfish (a type
of carp) live off the
plants that grow on the
river's bed and banks.

FISH DEFENSES

As well as finding enough to eat, fish must try to make sure that they aren't eaten themselves. Many fish do this by hiding themselves. Flatfish, which live on the bottom of the sea, have colored markings that blend in with the seabed. The fish can actually change the shape and color of its **camouflage** markings to suit the background it finds itself against.

Many ocean-swimming fish have dark-colored backs and silvery bellies and sides. This makes them very difficult to see from above, where they blend with the dark ocean, or from below, where they blend with the light from the sky.

Some types of fish camouflage themselves by looking like seaweed. Others look like dead leaves floating on a river. Still other fish look like rocks.

Some fish appear to be dangerous when they are not. One type of eel looks just like a poisonous sea snake. Weever fish, which often lie half buried in the sand, have poisonous spines on their gill

▼ Stonefish *(top)* are difficult to see. They also have poisonous spines.

▼ This Sargassum fish *(center)* looks just like a piece of seaweed.

◄ The anemone fish is protected by the stinging tentacles of the sea anemone.

flaps. They will raise these poisonous spines if they are disturbed. Sole don't have poisonous spines, but they pretend that they do by raising a fin.

Many fish protect themselves by making themselves difficult to eat. Puffer fish and porcupine fish have strong spines on their skin. If they are attacked they make themselves much bigger than normal by swallowing huge amounts of water so that the spines stand out.

There are also fish that are very poisonous. Weever fish have already been mentioned; they are poisonous enough to kill a human. Several other kinds of fish, such as toadfish and stonefish, are just as dangerous.

▲ This spiny puffer fish has made its spines stand out to protect itself.

▼ A leaf-fish is well camouflaged on the seabed.

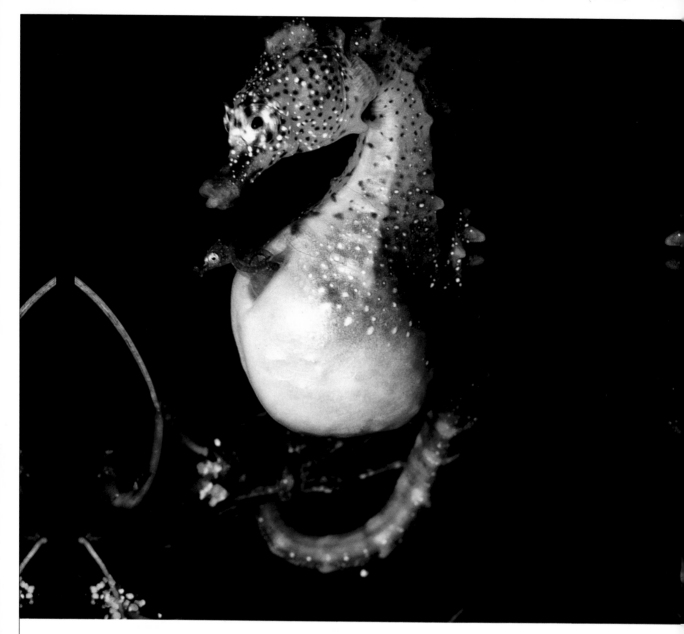

THE NEXT GENERATION

▲ Tiny seahorses emerge from an adult male's pouch.

Most female fish lay eggs, often in very large numbers. In order for young fish to develop inside the eggs, the eggs must be fertilized by a male fish. In a few cases, this takes place before the eggs are laid, but for most fish the eggs are fertilized by the male after they have been laid.

The eggs of many fish simply float freely, unprotected, in the ocean. This means that many of them are eaten by other fish. Some kinds of fish hide their eggs in mud at the bottom of rivers or make a nest for them. A male seahorse gathers up the fertilized eggs and keeps them safe in a pouch on his belly while they grow. Mouthbrooders collect their eggs and carry them around in their mouths until they hatch.

A very few kinds of fish, whose eggs are fertilized inside the female, give birth to live young – for instance, many sharks.

Some fish can actually switch between being male and female. As they grow older they may change from males into females. Others are both male and female at the same time and are able to fertilize their own eggs. Tripod fish, which live on the bottom of the ocean, are like this. Perhaps this is because it is difficult to find a mate in the darkness!

A male anglerfish, another deep-sea fish, is able to find a female by smell. When he does find a female, the small male fish attaches himself to her by his mouth. He remains attached to her for the rest of his life. This means that the female never has to look for a male to fertilize her eggs.

▲ Young rainbow trout hatching from their eggs.

▼ As the female brown trout lays her eggs, the male trout swims beside her to fertilize them.

27

A WATERY WORLD

Fish have been swimming in the waters of the world since before the time of the dinosaurs. There are fish in nearly all parts of the ocean, from the blackest depths to the sunlit coral reefs. Fish are also found in rivers and lakes. Every year new kinds of fish are discovered.

It is difficult to sum up in a few words what a fish actually is. All fish live in water and breathe through gills. They all have fins to help them move about. Most fish have a lateral line sense, but some other water-living animals do as well.

Only fish have swim bladders, but not all fish do. Most fish lay eggs, but some do not.

The lives of fish and the ways in which they are suited to their watery world are complex and fascinating. So is their vital role in the web of life. Fish depend on other water-living animals and plants for their own survival and in turn provide food for many birds and other animals, including humans. There is still much to understand about fish and their place in our living world.

▼ Fish can be found in almost all of the world's watery places. Here, sea goldfish swim through the coral of the Red Sea.

INDEX